EASY PIANO

POPULAR P...

10 TIMELESS CHRISTIAN WORS...

INTERMEDIATE TO LATE INTERMEDIATE PIANO SOLOS

ARRANGED BY BRYCE INMAN

ALFRED

Produced by
Alfred Music Publishing Co., Inc.
P.O. Box 10003
Van Nuys, CA 91410-0003
alfred.com

Printed in USA.

ISBN-10: 0-7390-6991-8
ISBN-13: 978-0-7390-6991-2

Cover Credits
Cross: © stock.xchng/natebernar   Sky: © stock.xchng/Mattox

Amazing Grace
(My Chains Are Gone)

Words and Music by
Chris Tomlin and Louie Giglio

Arranged by Bryce Inman

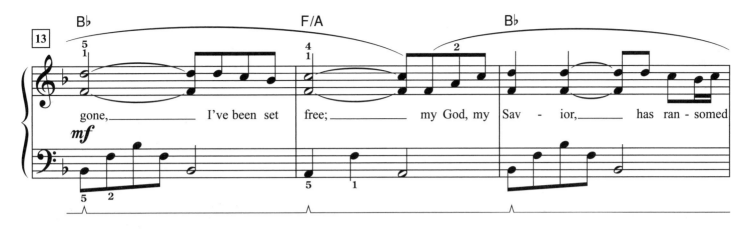

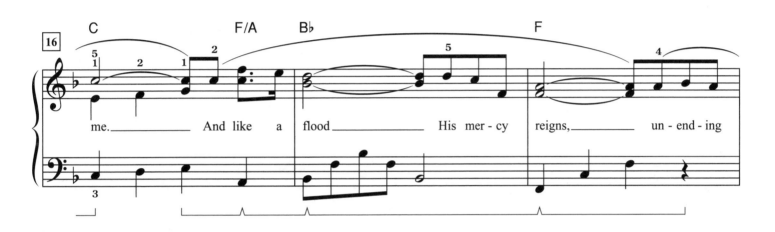

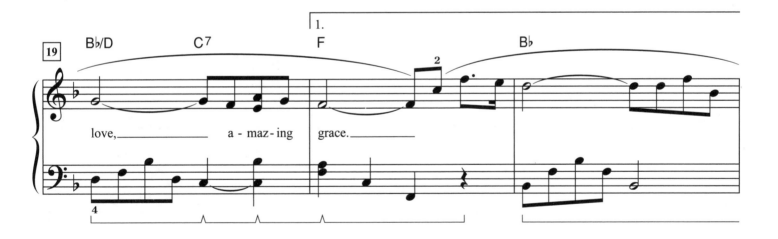

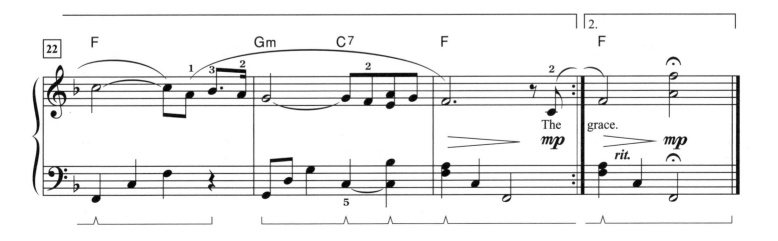

Blessed Be Your Name

Words and Music by
Beth Redman and Matt Redman

Arranged by Bryce Inman

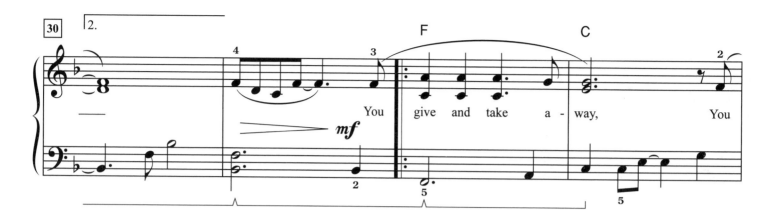

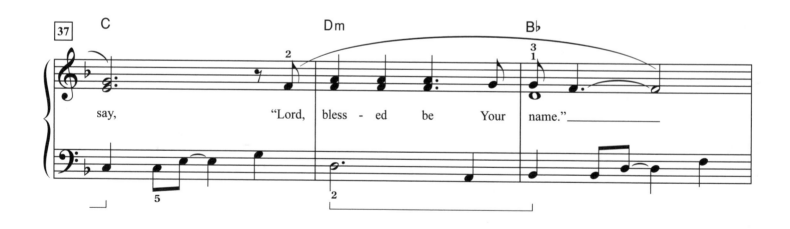

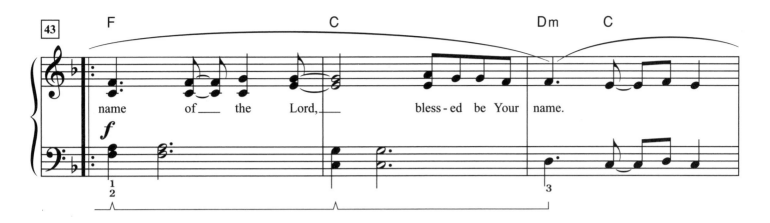

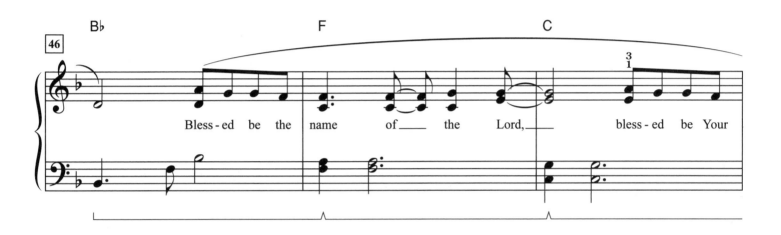

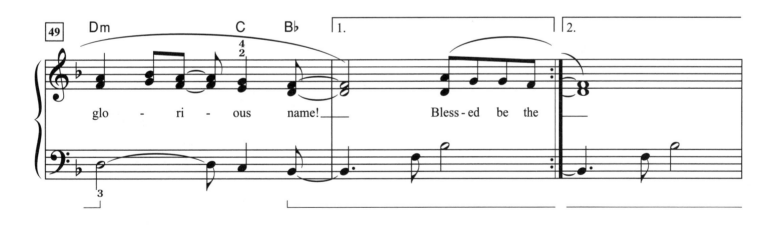

Come, Now Is the Time to Worship

Words and Music by Brian Doerksen
Arranged by Bryce Inman

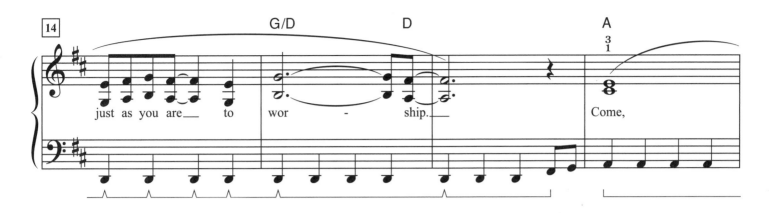

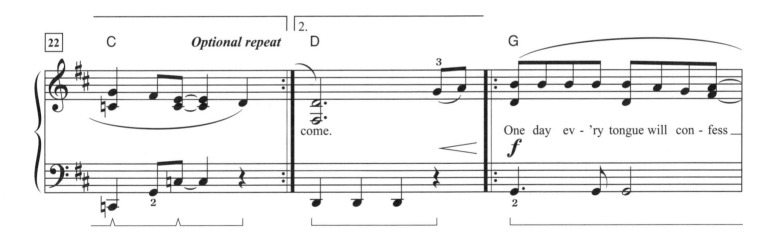

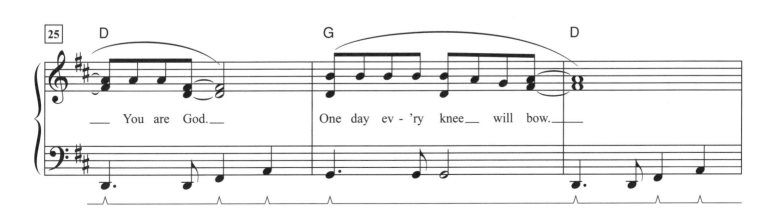

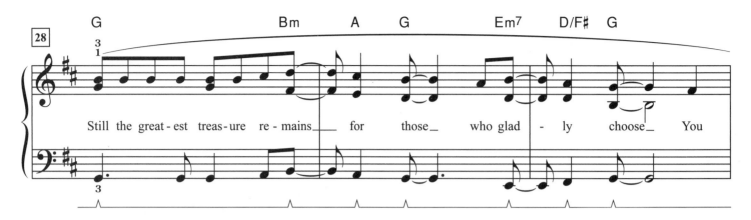

Still the great-est treas-ure re-mains___ for those___ who glad - ly choose___ You now.

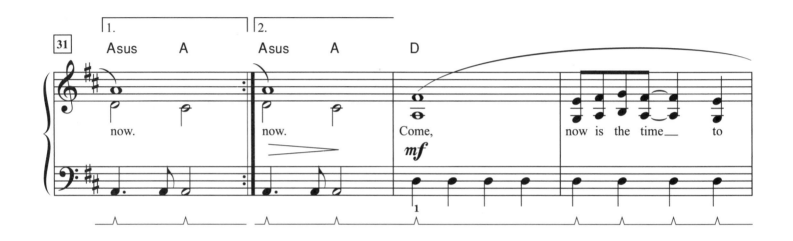

now. now. Come, now is the time___ to

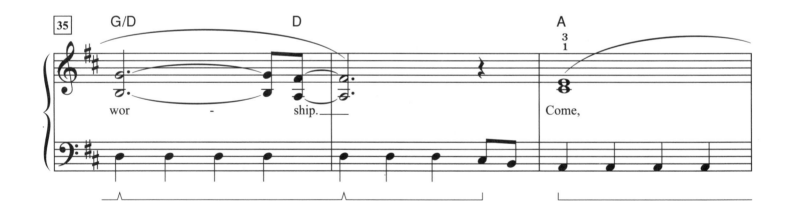

wor - ship.___ Come,

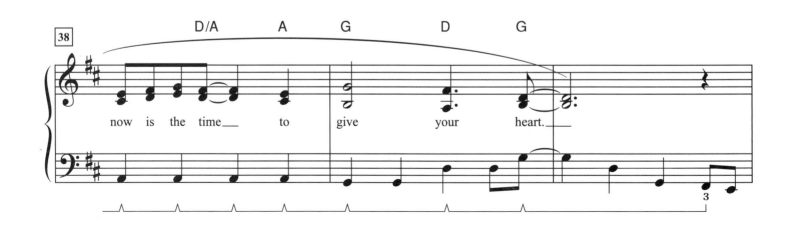

now is the time___ to give your heart.___

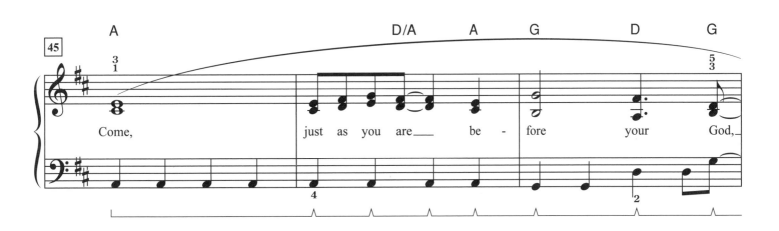

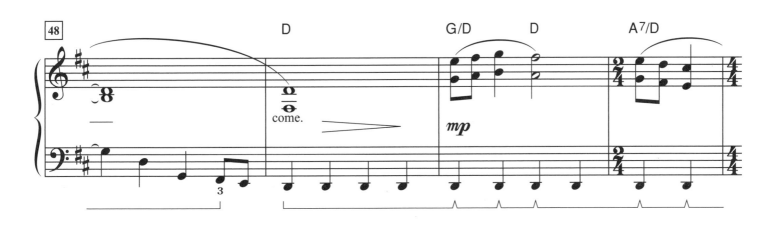

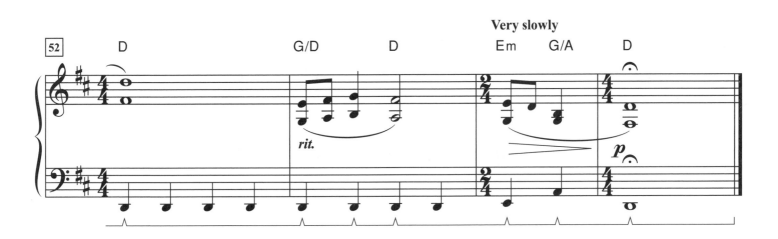

Beautiful One

Words and Music by Tim Hughes

Arranged by Bryce Inman

Forever

Words and Music by Chris Tomlin
Arranged by Bryce Inman

Moderately fast, with energy ($\quarternote$ = 112)

Give thanks to the Lord,__ our God and King.__ His
might - y hand__ and out-stretched arm,__ His

love en - dures__ for-ev - er.
love en - dures__ for-ev - er.

For He is good,__ He is a -
For__ the life_____ that's

bove all things.__ His love en - dures__ for-ev - er._____ Sing
been re - born,__ His love en - dures__ for-ev - er._____

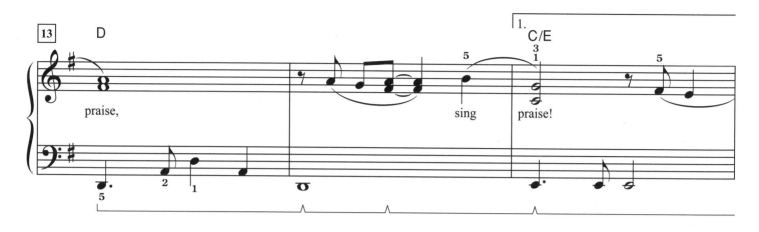

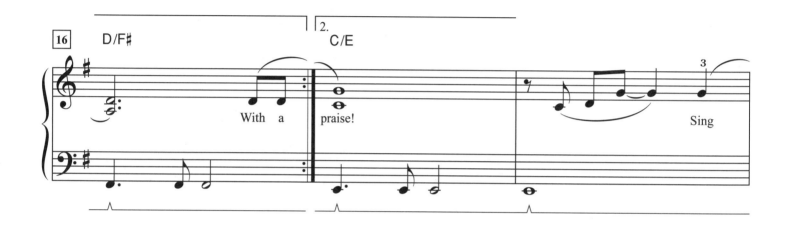

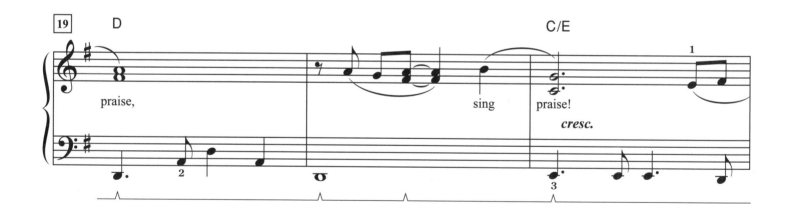

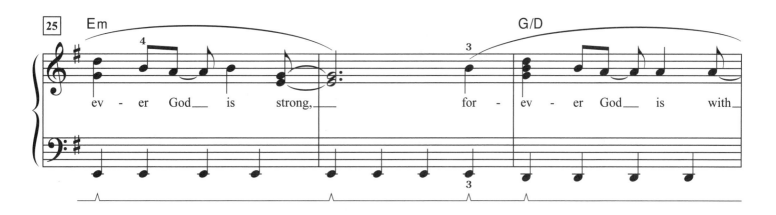

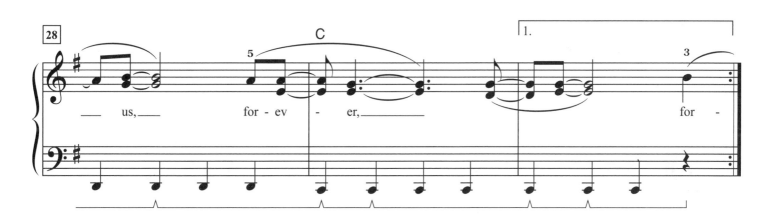

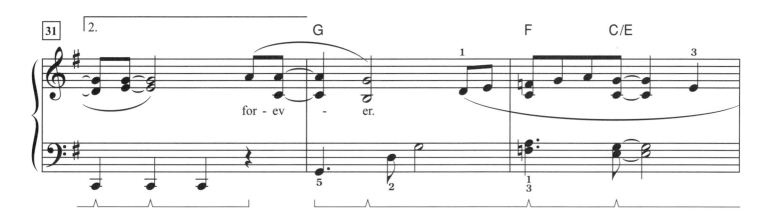

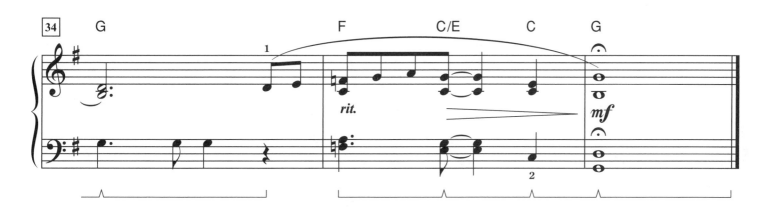

Here I Am to Worship

Words and Music by Tim Hughes
Arranged by Bryce Inman

How Great Is Our God

Words and Music by
Jesse Reeves, Chris Tomlin and Ed Cash
Arranged by Bryce Inman

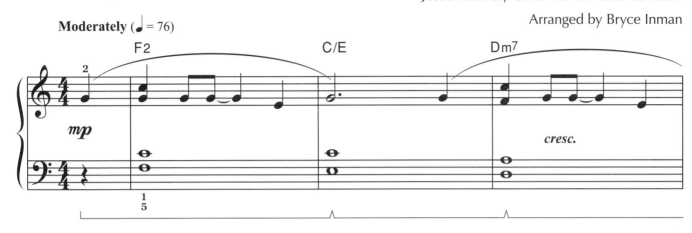

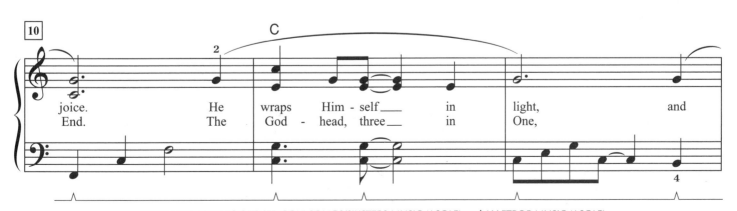

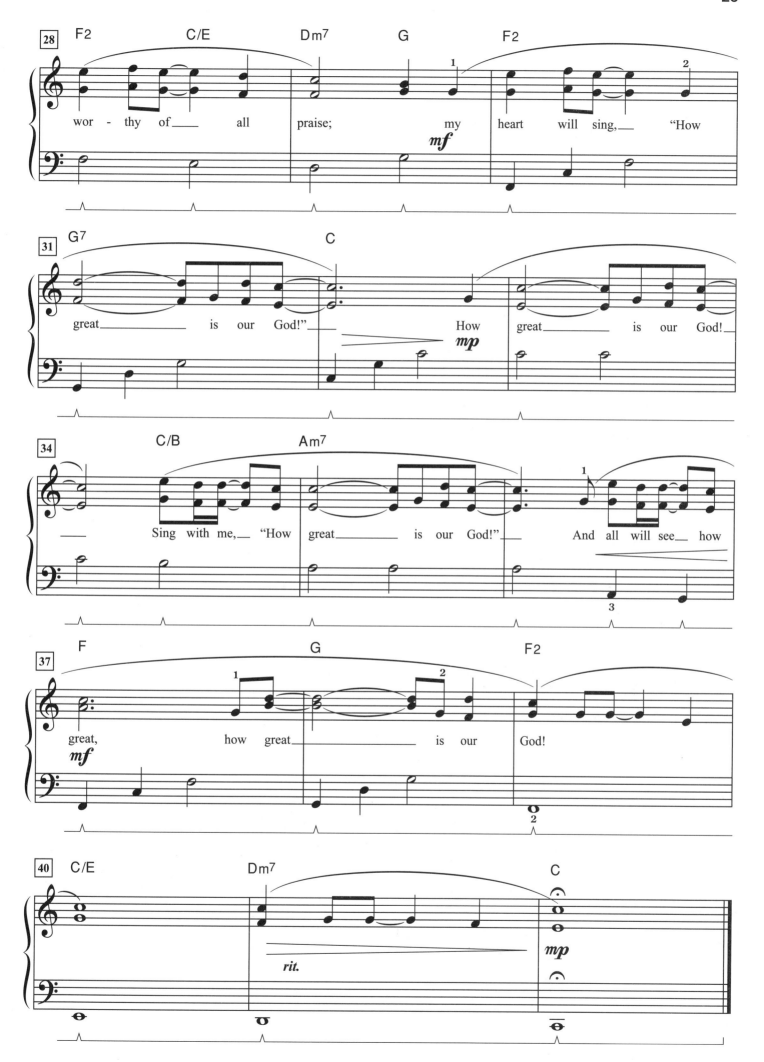

In Christ Alone
(My Hope Is Found)

Words and Music by
Stuart Townend and Keith Getty

Arranged by Bryce Inman

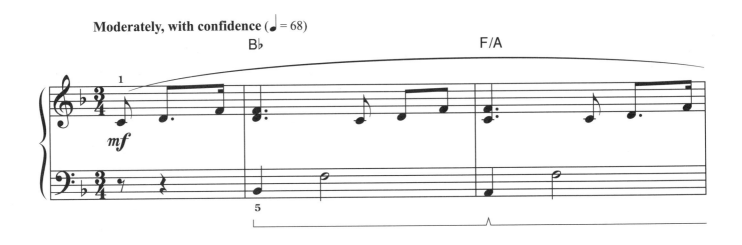

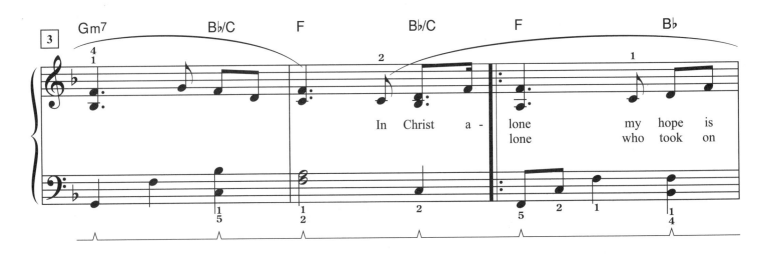

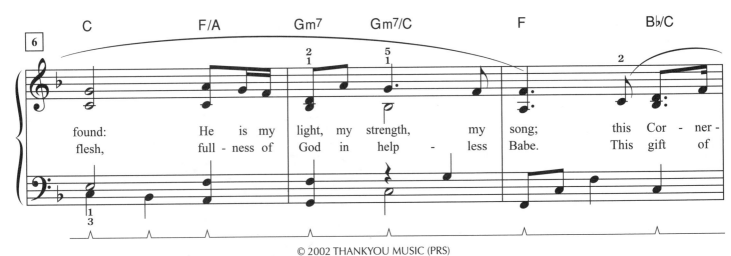

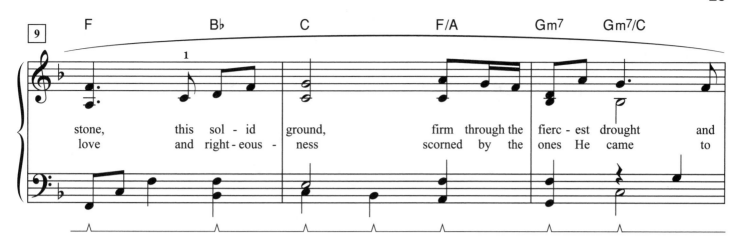

stone, this sol - id ground, firm through the fierc - est drought and
love and right - eous - ness scorned by the ones He came to

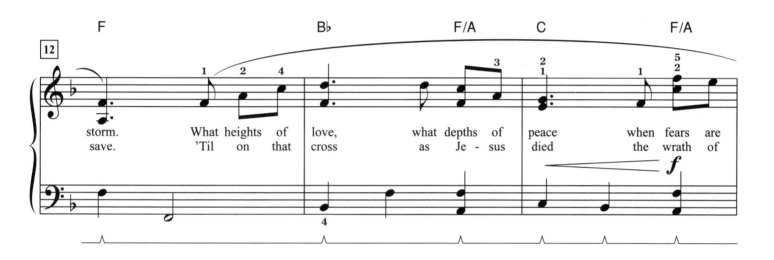

storm. What heights of love, what depths of peace when fears are
save. 'Til on that cross as Je - sus died when the wrath of

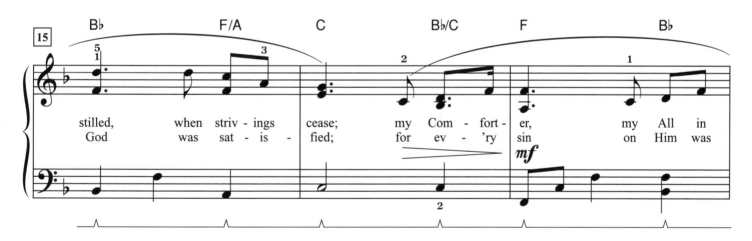

stilled, when striv - ings cease; my Com - fort - er, my All in
God was sat - is - fied; for ev - 'ry sin on Him was

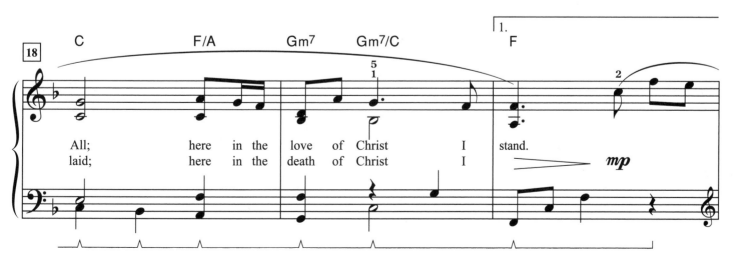

All; here in the love of Christ I stand.
laid; here in the death of Christ I

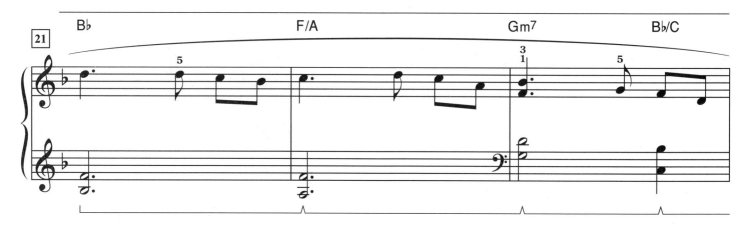

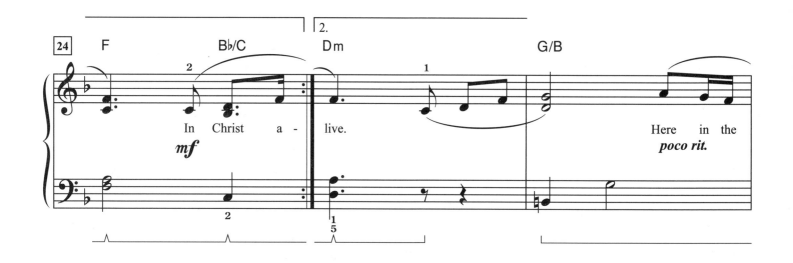

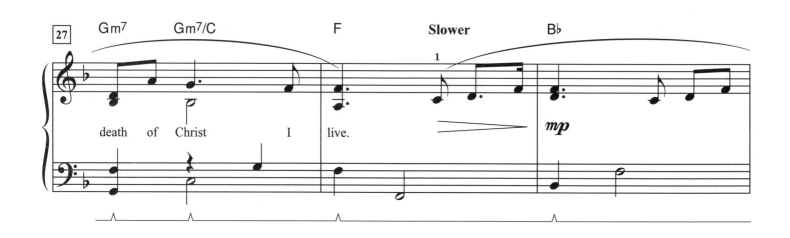

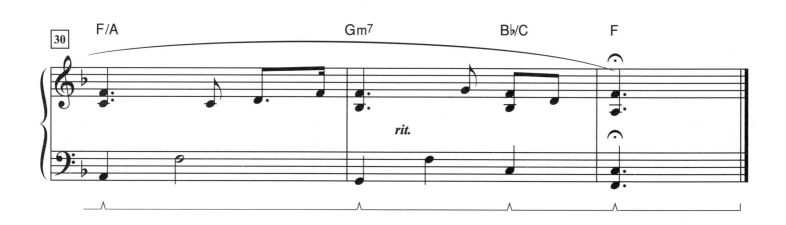

You Are My All in All

Words and Music by Dennis L. Jernigan
Arranged by Bryce Inman

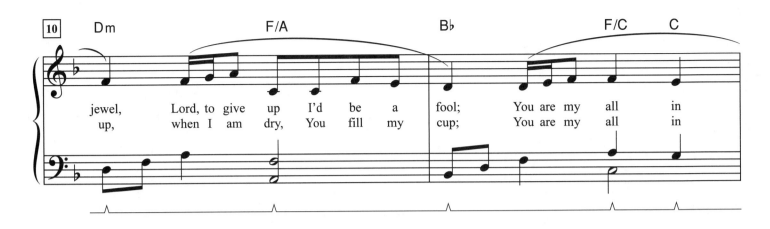

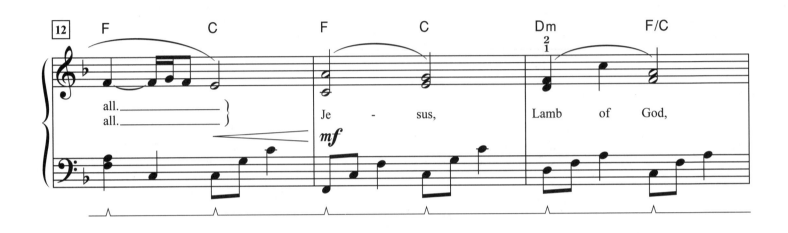

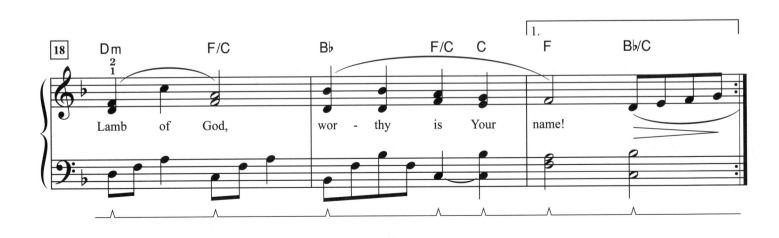

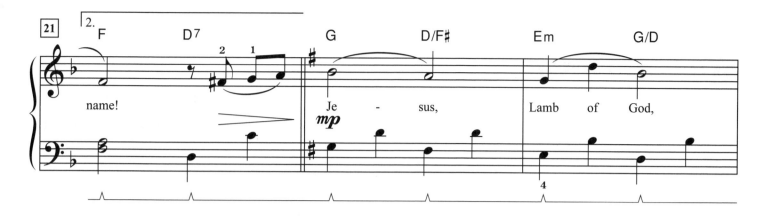

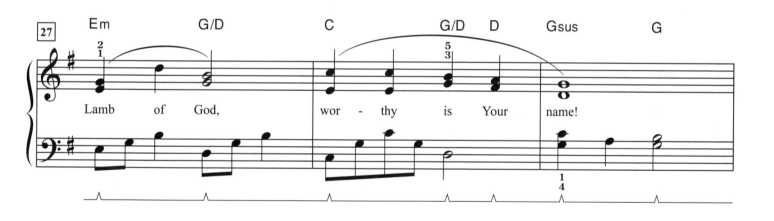

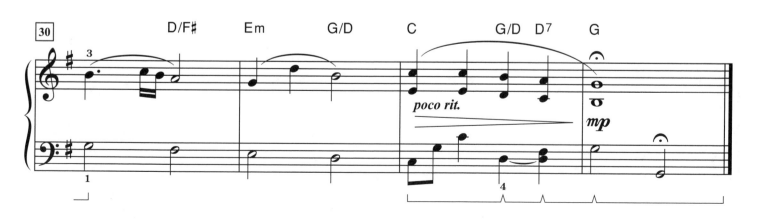

We Fall Down

Words and Music by Chris Tomlin

Arranged by Bryce Inman